MOTORCYCLE HAIKU 4

The Next Adventure
of Lobo Solitario
in Noir et Blanc

MARK FARGO

The Art of
Motorcycle Haiku
Moto Poet Mark Fargo's
Anthology
Reveals More Road Discoveries
MARK FARGO

MOTORCYCLE
HAIKU
Lobo Solitario Mark Fargo shares images
from his travels through Haiku Poetry

MOTORCYCLE
HAIKU
DÉJÀ VU
Moto Poet Mark Fargo
continues his photo Haiku journeys.

I'M JUST AN
OLD
BEATNIK
MARK FARGO

EARLY
MORNINO
OFFERINGS
A BOOK OF BEATNIK POETRY
Mark Fargo

MOTORCYCLE HAIKU 4

MARK FARGO

ISBN 978-1-959457-16-9

Book Design by Blue Jay Ink
Ojai, California
bluejayink.com

Published in the United States by
Lone Wolf Prints in association with Blue Jay Ink

markfargo.com

"When you ride a motorcycle, you have to be a
defensive rider. You've got to be a defensive driver.
You don't have time to talk on the phone, you don't
have time to eat."

Michael Jordan
April 11, 2021
NBA Hall of Fame 2009

My Mantra

Motorcycling is a privilege, not an entitlement.
You have to respect the road that many others don't.
You're invisible to many, some see you late and
others don't care. Constantly be scanning, use your
side view mirrors and be ready to react. It's about
your love for riding and survival. Any freedoms we
all enjoy cannot be taken for granted.

courtesy of Greg Gottlieb

Moto Poet: A lone traveler who combines photography and poetry to record his journeys.

Special note.

Let's be clear on one specific point. I write my Haikus in my form of the English language. The traditional 5-7-5 format. Traditional Japanese Haiku is written in one line vertically and addresses a season or change of seasons. That being said, I adapted the cultural Japanese format to fit my format.

Prologue

Noir et Blanc

For over eight years now, me and my whatever new model iPad, yes iPad, have traveled all over the country a handful of times, riding just three motorcycles in that period and spending a great amount of time in the western and Midwestern States, racking up tens of thousands of miles, about a hundred and twenty thousand of them just on my Yamaha Super Tenere. I am blessed to be healthy and have a reliable motorcycle to accompany me.

I've always wondered what some of the great color images I have would look like in black and white but never investigated that possibility because the response from my humble cult of color pictures followers were constantly telling me "Great shot, Mark," or "Love that shot, where did you take it?" What camera did you use? I always try to be humble and remind everybody the lens is just a reflection of my eye and I don't take the shot, the camera does - I just push the button. I often made up an imaginary camera model no one had heard of just to see if anybody cared. Non-photography people and fans of my adventures didn't question anything, but people engaged in photography would often respond, WHAT? Are you sure you got the right model name and number? "There's no such device, Mark." I would quickly get reprimanded and reminded, in a friendly manner, that there's no such camera on this beautiful planet. Ha! I'm busted!

The lenses on today's cameras are exceptional and people are now shooting movies on their phones and getting great reviews! I still have an iPhone 8 and see no reason to give up one of my retirement investments to own the iPhone 14 Pro Max. I'm kind of tech challenged to begin with, so many people telling me I need this or that new gadget makes me less interested in getting one. I'm sure some day I'll be back to a flip phone or something less simple like Agent Maxwell Smart's shoe phone. It's safe to say I'm not going to record my road life with the latest Go Pro helmet camera. My life is not a reality show, its just me living my life in the moment.

Regarding my use of an iPad instead of a camera with multiple lenses, filters and God knows what newly discovered technology to create better images, this was never an option for me because of the way I approach my daily travels and photography from my two wheeled companion, aptly named "Lobo Solitario"… Lone Wolf. I need to see the whole picture in a large lens to assess my point of interest and the iPad is perfect for my needs. I am often getting off my ride several times a day to capture a fleeting image from the landscape. Imagine all the procedural practices one goes through just to set up the traditional camera shot. It takes sometimes thirty minutes to adjust for the light! All the covers of my books would have disappeared getting ready for the shot if I had used all that time to get ready. I'm spontaneous, but sometimes it does take a long time to get the shot I want, especially if If I'm waiting for some shadows to work their magic.

Many of my shots would be gone if I took all that time to get set up. Photography for me is like the Haiku I write for the images, often spontaneous and with interesting and great results. Some Haikus drive me nuts, though, because of their traditional 5-7-5 syllable format, which I honor. Sometimes one syllable short, sometimes one too many. I really don't consider myself a photographer, but rather a traveler who has a good eye for the landscape. People win photography contests with their phones, so no offense taken. No contests for me. A gallery showing someday would be great!

When I was in Yosemite in the late fall of 2021, I went on a private guided tour of some of Ansel Adams favorite spots for his images: the great valley floor, El Cap, Tunnel View and Half Dome, just to name a few. One of my childhood friends, Greg Gottlieb, successfully navigates all those lenses, filters and F stops, unlike me. We have two totally different approaches to photography, but we respect how the other approaches it. He's not interested in the daily challenges of being on two wheels, and I'm not interested in lugging around some big bulky case of equipment. What we do have in common is our love for landscape photography and The Dodgers.

Our knowledgeable guide in Yosemite was Michael Wise, who told us the biggest obstacle to a good photograph is the photographer's ego. Sometimes when one starts getting recognition and selling their work, their quality of work goes south. Do it because you love doing it and if something comes from it, it's icing on the cake. I'm not sure if I'm interested in going to the next level, with all the complications and adjustments, it isn't worth the investment. I don't plan to make any changes anytime soon. I'm a motorcyclist first, poet next, and then landscape photographer.

Mike emphasized that photography is what you really want, and your best work will shine brightly. There wasn't much I could say about the technical part of setting up the camera. But Mike saw some of my work, liked it, and said to just keep doing what I was doing. It was well worth the time and money to see how Ansel approached his work.

Yosemite, frankly, is one of my favorite places on this earth. Those granite rocks, its massive walls and brilliant landscapes humble me, and I hope that valley never changes. I am devoting several images of Yosemite in this book.

Now there are exceptions, like trying to get that precise moment when the sun kisses El Cap and Half Dome in Yosemite at the same time at a location called Tunnel View. People come from all over the world for that one shot. These people are checking all their devices to see the exact time that moment happens. It takes some of these photographers at least an hour to set things up. People sleep in their cars and vans to jostle for the best position to wait, with their coffee, to be ready for "the shot." It takes me one minute to get set up but possibly an hour squatting in a spot for the shot. I know what I'm doing. I hear some people get there hours before in the dark for that last parking spot. Like a rock concert with no reservations, you get there early and bring your coffee and binoculars. Depending on the time of year, it's a war out there. In November 2021, it wasn't the cars and finding a parking space that was the issue, but two straight days of cloud cover that prevented me from "getting the shot."

It was never my intention to get too involved investing in expensive equipment, as it's constantly changing and the money hole it creates in your wallet just gets deeper. Some people's tripods cost more than my Air 3 iPad! I don't begrudge their path, but when you're on a motorcycle, traveling all over the country, you try to limit your bike weight and must compact all your gear. My device also has a keyboard which is great for me. It allows me to connect Haiku with images that same day and it's one less piece of gear I have to carry. My daily experience is my life and sharing it with you is my goal. The many compliments I get are my motivation to continue my quest for the rewarding results I strive for and often receive.

I get many interesting comments regarding my ride. Yamaha's Super Tenere is by far, in my opinion, the most practical and affordable dual sport motorcycle on the road. Geez, I have to change the damn oil every four to five thousand miles. Come On Man! I also have blistered my front windshield with reflective yellow tape (27 pieces). Last time I checked, with the red boxed out tape on my panniers on the back, I have over eighty pieces of tape on my ride. This enables me to be seen about a hundred yards away day or night by oncoming traffic and has saved hundreds of dollars in added gadgets costs. I get many smiles, questions and compliments from law enforcement, motorcyclists, and others from all walks of life when they see my ride. I've had tons of parking lot conversations, none of them negative. Most say I'm smart for making myself more visible for the growing number of impaired drivers out there. Technology has been one of the main culprits in this past generations of motorcycle fatalities.

Despite all that attention, I have not seen that reflective look all these years on the road. I'm a one-offer, I guess, and never apologetic about it. I can't emphasize how important safety is to me. I've recently added some very functional high end amber running lights for even more visibility. Some say I look alien like, and others have asked if I had someone do the artwork. From the front, my ride looks very cool and usually makes people slightly pause, which is exactly what my purpose is, to make people slow down and reflect on what's coming their way. It's especially effective at night on poorly lit two-lane highways which might have nonverbal four-legged beasts dashing across the pavement or the unfortunate drunk driver, who has two legs but a two-thousand pound truck to protect them. There have been some close calls out there, too many for me to keep track of. My instincts are my best asset.

One article written about my travels referred to me as Ego Solum Iter, Latin for, I Travel Alone. I've discussed this in my other books so just a quick reference as to why I do. I didn't start riding and shooting pictures until I was over sixty years old. With Sturgis and other "You have to do this ride or event" not an option nor of any interest for me, traveling alone is my key to freedom every day I'm out there. I don't have to answer to anything or anyone but the challenging weather and poor drivers' behavior. You live your choices so there is no excuse for failure. Motorcycling is a privilege, not an entitlement, so I have deep respect for the road and my surroundings, never taking anything for granted. I always wear a helmet because that's a no brainer, pun intended.

I don't spend a lot of time reading and assessing other people's work. I feel one needs to develop his own style and leave it to the public to do the assessing. Favorable responses at readings and books signings for me lets me know I'm on track presenting my photos, poetry and reflections. That doesn't mean I'm going to make a living doing it. Most people just entering the business of publishing, like I was seven years ago, get trapped into thinking companies are a cure all to selling books. I realized that by the time I retired at sixty-three, after two successfully reviewed Beat poetry books but not many sales, I was just a sitting duck for a barrage of marketing phone calls. The usual product out there will cost at least a thousand dollars to develop a plan for competing with the other eight million authors on the market. What is really annoying is that some publishers mentioned that my book received positive reviews from their team. I have five books, two Beat and three Motorcycle Haiku in the can, but they often don't even mention WHICH book it is that they have reviewed. Yikes! People, do your homework.

I feel really privileged spending an average of over eleven months on the road battling all the possible conditions locally to get a glimpse of our beautiful but socially challenging country that we all love. I don't spend any time staring at a GPS device on my handlebars or checking weather updates. I usually do that at home before I leave. That information doesn't always give the most accurate updates. I expect that when I'm in the Midwest, especially in the summer and fall, an occasional monsoon shower will hit me, and the deluge will force me off the road. Other times, I know ahead of time what I'm in for. One example comes to mind when leaving Portland, Oregon, in the late summer of 2021 enroute to Crescent City, California. A solid easy one-day ride of about three hundred and thirty miles. I'm seeing some moderate to heavy rain cells along that route. Most experienced riders know they can handle a few hours of nature's dowsing.

All those pesky weather cells must have all contacted one another as I was, for over nine hours, soaked and only stopping for gas and some food, riding in moderate to heavy rain the whole way. It was the worst experience of my whole motorcycling life. Even with rain gear, I became a drenched rat soaked from the neck down. All that water from the road just rode right on up my legs and as I suspected, my waterproof jacket was just water resistant. I also forgot my water-proof gloves, so I rode gloveless, which added to my misery. My hands were kind of a mushy pod of buttered toast. Ha. That's totally on me, but most gear is not going to put up with that amount of water for all those hours. By the time I got to Crescent City, which was clearing, I was exhausted! I peeled my clothes off at the hotel and got into dry clothes after a ten-minute hot shower. I had to get to the laundromat early as I was on my last pair of dry and clean clothes. Lesson learned, and don't repeat mine, please!

Recently, in the fall of 2022, I was subjected to a dime size hail storm with no town in sight, no abandoned buildings or coverings nearby. Many will boast that ain't nothing compared to golf ball sized hail pounding their WINDSHIELDS of their car. Oh, you were in a car…mmmmmm. When you're only covered by a helmet and what you're wearing, it's loud and it stings. I didn't have my weatherproof gloves on since there was no storm brewing from my last check. I couldn't see a thing, but just used my instincts, following the taillights in front of me. Twenty miles later the storm broke and I could breathe again. When I got to a hotel, I created my own lake waiting in the lobby with five other people wanting a room. I was inconsistently shaking in one place, but just happy to be in a warm building that had a roof.

I hope you enjoy these images, Haiku, and short vignettes, in this, my fourth installment of Motorcycle Haiku, Noir et Blanc.

My website, markfargo.com, has a collection of current Beat Poetry as well as where and how to purchase my latest work. I am grateful for all of you who have supported me all these years. As long as I can physically ride, expect the photos, Haiku, and books to continue.

Past Images

After gathering pictures, writing the Haikus and vignettes, and producing this book, I have wondered what my past images from my previous works would look like in black and white. As a bonus, I have selected various photos with their Haiku, which I filtered in black and white. This enabled me to embrace what the black-and-white genre of this new book represents; simple but very distinct contrasts from color, and often powerful images, images shot now in black and white. Ansel had it right. Enjoy these reboots.

Dedication

The Grey Panther

Ahead of her time
More qualified than most men
Loved by all my friends

My mom, Cecilia, was among the proud fighters for women's rights in the early seventies. It was always about who's qualified not what gender you were. Never burned her bra or hated men and outlived all her beloved cats. Despite me being me, believed in me even when I didn't.

Charles

Tuff love growing up
Too old school for your three wives
Cancer took you fast
Glad I got some of your DNA
Wish we had more time to mend

His education was from the school of Hard Knox. He meets my UTEP and Stanford educated bilingual mother. Both are well groomed and fit. My dad is a charmer but has already had children from two different women. I'm surprised that these polar opposites stayed together for seventeen years. We had a stressful relationship I wish would have ended on a more positive note.

Passing Loved Ones
(Tankas)

Tanka for Cindi

Cancer has no friends
No complaints along the way.
Loved her Boys in Blue
Years of treatment and rebound
Won the battle lost the war

Lance

Happy he was picked
At the door when we got home
Tail always wagging
Ear shattering chalk board bark
His final road trip now done

RD

Books guns native lore
Smoking watching old westerns
I called him cowboy
Bad guy rolls, some people died
Austere presence, heart of gold.

Montalvo Mayor

Accordion king
Alameda fun and games
Back stairs church smoking
Van rockin' don't come knocking
Tough guy face but smiling heart.

Marmalade

Hospice last request
Orange tabby rescue for mom
Loved daily brushing
Iron gate haven from dogs
Miss her chatty love call song

Ame Moulette

Jamala Beach site
Winds unusually calm
His perch his castle

The sensuous two lane road that leads to Jamala Beach is pretty well paved with some bad patches, some S turns and a little gravel along the way. It's fifteen miles off of Highway 1 on the way to Vandenberg Air Force Base. Plenty of RV and campsites. Usually windy and home to the famous Jamala Burger, which if you're a fan of the cow, a must meal you'll enjoy.

The Falls

Upper and lower
Surrounded by granite walls
Majestic icon

*Yosemite National Park is by far a must visit on your bucket list. The Valley is immense and you start your first hike at 4,000- feet so take one day to adjust if so inclined. The sheer granite walls, the waterfalls and indigenous wildlife are something worth your time. My favorite park in the United States. ****For your own mental health, go in the off season.*

Goleta Beach

Is it day or night?
is it the sun or full moon?
Ocean face shimmering

*The frontage road running north of Goleta beach stops at one of
the entrances to Hollister Ranch where some of my Buena High
School alum use to take boats from into for some great surfing.
This shot just appeared out of nowhere as I was just hanging
around waiting for something to appear.*

Desert Chief

Prominent forehead
Sharp pointed nose high cheekbones
Sage and cacti lay

Famed Indian Head in the state's largest park, Anza Borrego (almost 600,000 acres) is one of my new favorite places to visit annually now. Bordered by the Colorado River and Salten Sea, it offers original palm trees to the state as well as some wonderful Badlands. Your late spring, summer and early fall visit will be a little toasty (in the 100 degree plus zone).

Abandoned

Decades of neglect
No license or registration
Safe haven for some

While in eastern Tennessee seeing on old childhood friend, Jvey Petro and his lovely wife Marti, we did a day trip to a fall festival in Pigeon Forge for some whiskey sampling. After my ten half shot sampling, a back road home to discover this gem.

Undisputed

Silos just watching
Two hundred tons of power
Owns the rails all day

While visiting my son Matt, his wife Shannon and my two grandchildren, Ryker and Maya, in Alton, Iowa, in the fall of 2022, I took advantage of this idling locomotive. The Mill was his but the silos belong to someone else. Lots of trains in the Midwest and a few million corn fields. Don't forget to stop in Matt's joint, Sumato Pizza, the best Neapolitan pizza you'll ever eat.

Stairway To...

Lighthouse decaying
Time and weather took its toll
Fresnel lens idle

I love lighthouses like at Point Reyes in California, where you walk down about three hundred steps to a very quaint gift shop and light house you can go into. This staircase was a shot I took at Oregon's Cape Blanco State Park in the summer of 2022. Beautiful area, campgrounds, some fog and extensive tide pools. It's like the old adage, from the ground up.

Repelling Nirvana

High desert climbing
Crooked River Calderon
Sheer cliffs basalt tuff

Smith Rock is the second most popular rappelled rock in the West and United States outside of Yosemite. It's located outside of Redmond in central Oregon near Bend. There is a unique limited open site campground I've stayed in the past couple of years where you must park about fifty years away from the parking lot and carry equipment in. No stoves allowed, though, as you must use common area for cooking etc. $8 a night, first come first serve.

Framed

Point Reyes Norcal
Dead cypress hug rugged coast
Cold winds embrace me

Point Lobo State Natural Reserve is a do-all with many sandy trails, sea loins and get gift shop. The Cypress there look so old and the dead ones frame many interesting spots to photograph. BUT….no dogs allowed on the trails and cannot be left in any vehicle.

The Icon

Ansel's favorite
Fall colors seasons changing
Merced River still

Half Dome was one of Ansel Adams favorite places to shoot his incredible imagery of Yosemite. It is reported, by our guide, he shot over five hundreds shots of it. I saw three different faces among my different locations. Ansel's work inspired me to go noir et blanc.

The Hunted

Rider of the storm
Black tunnel chasing me down
Let the games begin.

The Hunted. I am often challenged on my journeys to try to figure out how to outrun impending storms, some of which come at you quickly and without fanfare. I won this round on my way to Iowa to see my son Matt and other relatives. I've also lost my share of battles as well.

Cape Flattery

Makah native tribe
Pilot whales avoid orcas
Neah Bay their home.

Located on the continents most Northern point on a Indian reservation, you are treated to many great chances for unusual shots depending on the time of day and weather. I saw rocks entering the cove as Pilot Whales immediately. There are Orca's in these waters.

Driftwood Lookout

Drift wood framing beach
winds just a whisper today
ocean laps the shore

Some of these huge logs on Jamala beach on California's southern coast can turn into these wonderful surfaces of many shapes and hiding places for its inhabitants. It's like I've said many times on my posts, it's why I live in California, the most diverse state in America.

Whale Rock

Alone in the bay
North bound gray whale migrating
Pacific coast stop

I'm sure I'm not the only one who sees faces in clouds, rocks and food. This shot was outside of Crescent City in Northern California, which can stay foggy all day in some parts of the year. It caught my attention from the highway which is where most of my photographs originate from.

Survivor

Leather seating
Cheap plates and old silverware
Waitress say, "Pie Hon"

*I've been fortunate to ride the Route 66 pretty much in its entirety. Since
I have only been discovering the United States by motorcycle journey
for about nine years, I missed its glory days before the interstate system
eventually put it into the nostalgic category of American History. I
always seek diners on my travels for that Blue Plate Special. My first trip
here but not my last. Outside of Kingman on the way to California.*

Season's Change

Night has no colors
Silence from snowflakes peaceful
Christmas morning glory

Loloma Lodge along the McKenzie River off Highway 126 in southern Oregon was perfect for our family Christmas weekend. We all had cabins and woke up in the morning to this scene.

Golden Fields

Parted by asphalt
Golden sea of yellow for miles
Endless silent grains

Along Highway 97 in Oregon - this is one of the reasons why I'm still riding. I actually had no idea where I was until later. One of those when you're at the Y decisions. You lose track of time and location when you see this opportunity in front of your popping wide eyes. This is motorcycle Nirvana.

Partner

In my thoughts daily
She knows my love for the road
Forever grateful

It's hard for some to realize my independent ways have been with me my whole life. I didn't really settle down until I met Maggie at age forty six. We both like to travel but it was sad when she chose not to be part of THIS kind of adventure. I knew I had to do it. I knew the risks but the journey I couldn't pass up. Motorcycling saved me from myself and I hope you'll find your form of motorcycling in your life.

Barn Quilts

Geometric art
Mystery of their meaning
Countryside treasure

My nephew Chuck and his wife Kay, who designed the quilt, display their time consuming efforts on their family barn on their Iowa countryside property. This sign weighed over two hundred pounds and was a six foot square. Some are much larger. The Pennsylvania Dutch were known for their circular hex designs which told about family stories or conveyed various messages.

Rest Stop

Open range for miles
Broken fences with barbed wire
Dreaming in the weeds

I realized when I started riding I physically wasn't forty anymore nor fifty. Geez, I wasn't even sixty anymore. When you ride big at my age you need a nap to get through the day. A solid twenty minutes lying on any type of surface will do, even asphalt if that's all that's offered. Here in the weeds, a gentle breeze woke me.

Desert Communities

Polka dot foothills
Scattered homes in the vast sands
More clouds than people

My most seen landscape in California, with all its desert regions, would be this type of environment. Tons of clouds embraced by blue skies hovering over unincorporated towns. Old buildings and cars, a few businesses and a few dogs running on the property.

The Slugger

Oregon tide pool
Grassy and rocky hideout
Yellow giveaway

I put this slug, the Babe Ruth of slugs, right in the middle of the shot. Its bright orange size made it an easy point of reference. It was actually still partially covered by kelp. Shot was taken at Cape Blanco lighthouse in Oregon's south coast area.

Bakers Delight

Stark summer setting
Patches of snow paint the peaks
Gloomy morning day

*In the Eastern Cascade mountains off Highway 20 in Washington,
is Mount Baker, elevation 10,781 feet. It's an active glacier-covered
andesitic stratovalcano. (Not sure what that means). It's the second most
active crater in the Cascade range after Mount St. Helens. I love its black
color, its darkness in the snow.*

Cadillac Graveyard

Caddies meet their faith
Dusty windy resting place
New paint job each day

Officially called Cadillac Palace, just west of Aramilio Texas, this is a family fun center to legally "graffiti" all you want with paint they sell there or like I did, just pick a can that's been left to leave your legacy, even if its temporary.

Pandemic

Beard longer than hair
Covid more time to reflect
thinking of the road

*During the height of the pandemic I decided to go rogue. This is the
trimmed down version of my Unabomber look. Some say this look
put me into a different class of motorcyclist, generically called a biker.
Appearance can be linked to the motorcycle you ride and vice versa.
There's no scientific study done, just people's perceptions. I ride alone and
will continue to have my own look. At the end of the day I'm still my
own club of one.*

Shaniko

Two stiffs on a bench
So what, my horse has two wheels
No, don't own a gun

Shaniko, population thirty six in the 2010 census, Oregon's best known ghost town in Waco County, was once a thriving transportation hub. Sheep, wheat and cattle were abundant . In the early 1900's Shaniko boasted being the largest wool warehouse in the state. A Union Pacific railroad subsidiary started using an alternate linking Portland to Bend which stared Shaniko decline. By 1966, the railroad was completely shut down. My last time through, I saw a goat waiting outside the entrance of the open post office.

Bad Boy's Tower

White gypsum jacket
Laccolithic butte
Phonolite columns

Lots of controversy trying to rename this site over the decades. I prefer to call it after what Native Americans would call it as opposed to The Devils Tower tag. I saw eagles flying above the rim. If I could, I would love to camp there one night.

Inclusion

Exiting tunnel
Neighborhood looks very mixed
Many shapes and sizes

It's not often I've seen this many different formations of rocks in such a small area. I usually see small or large bunches of families of the same demographic. This picture really does feel like it represents what America looks like today.

Earning My Keep

Great meal on the way
Thought I was just visiting
Dishwasher my choice

I have friends from my childhood now living elsewhere and have a few new ones I've made along the way. In many states now, I can wind down and settle in for a few great meals and sleep on a bed after a few long days in a tent camping on the road. (I have a 72 hour rule for visits). I earned both here but definitely earned my meal for the day at Coconut Joe's in South Carolina.

Desperate Times

High mountain deserts
Mormons seek new grazing lands
Water very scarce

Brigham Young in the 1870's miscalculated this site for his followers to settle with their livestock they had hoped could graze and thrive. The Castle Valley and the San Rafael Swell in south central Utah was very challenging and was not the lush pastureland they had hoped for.

Yosemite Spider

Walking on water
Logged tarantula resting
Destination beach

The Yosemite Valley offers so much to photographers, hikers, rock climbers and just curious tourists gasping at these sites for the first time. I've been there enough now to know it's my favorite National park in this country.

Tree Tunnel

Cold air calm waters
Portal to granite mountains
Landscape awaiting snow

Mid November 2021, one of my childhood friends and I went to Yosemite for some tent camping and to photograph the magnificent Yosemite Valley. It was just for three days and we got hundreds of stunning pictures. When I first saw that lone dark tree in the middle of the area I thought it was a portal to the mountain.

Sacred Place

Peacock guardian
Elaborate furnishings
Urban location

They place an awkward sign right in front of the temple so you can't really get a centered close up shot on purpose. A friend from South Carolina said it was something worth looking into. It was. This isn't South Carolina or India, it's Atlanta, Georgia.

Pegging

Not the Titanic
Ravishing young lady gone
Alone on the bow.

courtesy of Greg Gottlieb

When I get up on my side pegs, sometimes leaning up against my windshield, it is mostly to stretch my weary calves and legs. This position is seen more on off-road pounding topography bikes with knobby tires and a helmet video camera. That upright position I ride, with my legs bent back towards the back tire, can be done by much younger people all day long, but those two hour plus stretches I ride, I need to take a break. My seventy year old butt, despite a custom seat, is wearing out. I'm trying to limit myself to under four hundred mile days now and back to back five hundred-plus days are an anomaly.

I also do pegging to see over guard rails for the views along the occan, dusty deserts, mountain passes, animal alerts and to check out road distractions, which I do at various speeds. I'm in control and feel safe pegging even at seventy miles per hour.

I've been told that my plastered yellow reflective tape on my windshield and bright amber running lights can be distracting. Since 80 MPH is the new speed limit, maybe that's the point, to slow down those four-wheeled vehicles that are coming at me. I've also been told that my ride has an artistic or alien appearance to it and I do see people stare at me while they're walking towards me on the street. Lots of thumbs up, and once at a middle school crossing the guard did a shout out at me as I was stopped right in front of the crosswalk. She told me she appreciated the safety practice which appears to be a solo one in this country.

My Haiku reference to the Titanic is solely for visual teasing and is not for its end results.

Epilogue

As the years pass me by, I am more thankful each day that I can still ride all over the country and collect images of this great country. I've lived through the 60s with its political assignations, the Civil Rights Act, Man on the Moon, Vietnam, Disco (Yikes), Watergate, 911, January 6th and many more major events that have shaped and changed our cultural norms and civility towards one another. I hope this changes in my lifetime.

On April 28th, 2023, I'll be seventy, yes, the big 7-0. On that day, exactly six years ago, I bought my Yamaha Super Tenere, a 1200 cc no extra frills motorcycle. I do concede, however, that I have cruise control to help relieve the pain from my arthritic hands. I also had a custom seat made for my "where's my butt gone," which has now just morphed into a white slab of relaxed muscles. Showroom seats aren't really made for what I do: they're for weekend riders on their way to lunch. No problem with me, but long-distance riding is a totally different animal.

Many of you have told me that you have been living vicariously through my photographs, Haiku, vignettes and end-of-the-day travels postings. I appreciate all the kind words over the years and hope to continue to do so as long as I can respond to the ever-changing driving challenges many people in this county have. I hope to keep growing in my efforts to improve my work in all its areas and hope you come along with me as I continue to discover America, with all its challenges, and keep reaping its rewards in solitude, with my thoughts.
Go in Peace.
Mark Ego Solum Iter Fargo

Special thanks to Dr. Gary Delanoeye, my friend and thesis advisor at Antioch University in Santa Barbara, who had to painstakingly review my thesis back in 2010 and who took on the challenge here with my latest adventure into the English language. I still write from my Beatnik roots. Your knowledge and friendship will always be appreciated; and to Linda Howey, who added the finishing touches.

And also special thanks to Eli Rassibi, owner of Wheels in Motion in Chatsworth, CA, and his competent staff, who have keep me safe with their excellent service on my Super Tenere motorcycle over the past seven years.

Lobo Solitaro

Traveling beyond my territory
mate at home with pups
family to feed my mission
jagged mountains icy streams to cross
my own hunger I ignore

I am lone wolf in the wilderness
hours and miles terrain unfamiliar
two lane highway I cross
pause to see heat risen mirage
coming from the mountain pass
muffled sound I hear
lone rider appears

red wine helmet black leather jacket
blue jeans patched worn black boots
sun is setting silhouette draws slowly
cautiously I approach
his two wheeled Cherry Red ride stand down
he is sitting silently on a rock
motionless alligator lizard sunning
orange and red sunset carpet among darkening blue skies
is he a lone wolf as well?

silent stare I notice his silver hair
horseshoe down mustache stubbled face
grey blue eyes
strong jaw tanned face
his road sense fill my nostrils
lone wolf he is

bringing his plaid bag and blankets by the fire
throws some jerky my way water in tin bowl
curbing my grumbling pain
volumes spoken with no words
respectful stare eyes connect
I rest nearby for the night

I know this man
connected we are
sunrise we both move on
different paths we take...alone

Lobo.....my only tattoo and constant companion.

Photo credit: Greg Gottlieb

Special Tanka

One of my best childhoods friends, John "Buns" McCarthy, father passed away this past New Years Eve 2022. He was an exceptional man. He was hard working vocational blue collar guy we all loved. For those of us who had a tumultuous relationships with our own fathers, which I was one, he would have been the perfect replacement. He was caring and always had that famous grin on his weathered face. He is survived by his (equally wonderful New England accent) caring wife Nora and their four children. He was ninety seven.

Last Christmas

Loved by everyone
Plastered dry walls union man
Nora his life mate
His face was always smiling
The world has lost a great soul